# The Going In-House Handbook

## A Concise Guide to Making Big Career Changes

Susan Ellen Wolf

Scout Publishing Enterprises
2011

Disclaimer: All anecdotes included in this concise guide are fictional. Any similarity to any actual individual, situation or corporation is coincidental.

ISBN: 978-0-9848416-0-8

In loving memory of my father, Julius Wolf, who passed on his passion for learning from everyday experiences.

—SEW

# Contents

# How to Use This Concise Guide

*The Going In-House Guidebook* highlights the major factors that any professional will want to consider when evaluating a particular in-house opportunity.

I've organized the book so that you'll easily find exactly what you need, without being bogged down by a lot of irrelevant information. The topics are pertinent for professionals in all disciplines, including doctors, lawyers, accountants, engineers, and consultants.

For the most part, corporations are not inherently good or bad, and the same can be said for employment positions; what is true, however, is that a particular position at a particular corporation will be a perfect fit for one professional—and torture for another, equally talented professional. This concise guide is intended to assist professionals with the following:

- Identifying the information they will need to make a well-informed decision about a particular position, and

- Avoiding being surprised by aspects of a position after they have already started work.

Each chapter can be used on a stand-alone basis. For example, if you're a lawyer who specializes in executive compensation, you might skip Chapter Five, which covers compensation. On the other hand, if you've held many in-house jobs in the past and just want to make sure you haven't missed anything in negotiating a current offer, you may need to read *only* Chapter Five.

Each chapter includes a checklist highlighting key action items that you'll find useful in evaluating the issues covered in that chapter.

The Appendix is a checklist that summarizes the main factors covered throughout *The Going In-House Guidebook*.

# How to Tell If Going In-House Is Right for You

Making a change from a professional services firm to an in-house position may be the perfect choice for you. Or it may not. In order to help you arrive at a decision that you're confident is the best for you, it's important that you carefully consider the differences between the day-to-day practice in each environment.

Professionals often base their decision to change jobs on a single factor. They may become so excited by changing that one factor that they don't fully evaluate the full range of differences between their current and prospective environments. That's a big mistake.

Let's take the example of an accountant. Whether he works in a Big Four accounting firm or a corporation, the accountant will be applying accounting standards, such as GAAP or IFRS, to produce accurate financial statements. However, in most respects, the day-to-day practice in a firm is very different from that of a corporation. In a firm, each accountant is essentially a profit center, and his business is the accounting business, whereas an accountant in a corporation is overhead, and his business is the corporation's business. An accountant who enjoys being an expert in a narrow area might be best suited for either the national office of an accounting firm (where he could advise many companies in a variety of industries on issues in his area of expertise) or a very large corporation (where a full-time expert is needed to handle certain specific issues for dozens of subsidiaries and divisions). That same accountant might be dissatisfied in a smaller corporation with a leaner staff, where each accountant must handle general accounting matters in addition to his area of expertise.

Similarly, almost all medical doctors aspire to apply their knowledge to improve people's lives. In private practice, most doctors deal with a broad spectrum of issues involving both the wellness and the illness of their patients. In-house at a hospital, however, doctors may care for patients suffering an illness or injury, and may also be involved in quality processes for hospitalized patients, but it's likely they will have little opportunity to work with patients on wellness. In-house as the chief medical officer at a pharmaceutical company, the doctor may establish quality standards for research and labeling; help regulators understand the medical objectives, benefits, and risks of a drug; and help scientists and executives keep abreast of developments in medical science. But he'll have little or no patient contact. By contrast, in-house as the head of the corporate medical clinic at a large manufacturing company, the doctor may address wellness, occupational safety, and fitness issues.

Let's take this a bit deeper. Imagine that a doctor who's board-certified in internal medicine is considering a move from private practice to hospital practice. His primary objective is to get away from the pressures created by HMOs and insurers. In private practice, the doctor can't avoid these third parties because that's how he gets paid. But those same parties often make it difficult for him to administer the treatment he thinks will provide the best health outcome for a particular patient. In his new role as a hospital doctor, where he'll be paid a good salary directly by the medical center, the stress of dealing with HMOs and insurers will be eliminated. But there are a few other factors our doctor needs to consider. For example, will he miss being able to help his patients achieve their wellness goals over time, such as managing diabetes or lowering cholesterol? And how might cost pressures at the hospital impact his hospital practice? Thoroughly considering all relevant factors may lead the doctor to investigate additional practice alternatives that could also satisfy his primary objective, such as joining a concierge practice or working on clinical trials at the National Institutes of Health.

Or imagine a lawyer who's tired of the constant pressure to bill as many hours as possible and to bring in new clients. She's absolutely right in thinking that if she takes an in-house corporate position, she'll leave both of those pressures behind. But once at her new position, she'll undoubtedly experience different pressures, including tight budgets and a need to provide answers face-to-face, right away. As one lawyer put it, "It's really different when the business executive's office is just down the hall and he wanders in for advice."

When going in-house, it's important to fully understand other positions you might be asked to rotate through in order to advance in your career. Some corporations require a professional to gain experience in a wide variety of disciplines and/or in diverse geographical areas (overseas, for example), before moving into leadership roles. The major reasons for this policy are that it allows the global team to get to know and respect the professional before being asked to follow his lead, and ensures that he has enough perspective and experience to effectively handle a significant leadership role.

Some corporations will consent to a talented employee turning down such assignments if he/she is content to remain at their current level. Other companies, however, may need to free up mid-level positions to reward junior level high-performers, and would terminate an employee who isn't willing to take on a range of different assignments. Before you even consider becoming an in-house employee, it's essential that you understand your prospective employer's policies on rotational assignments.

Consider an accountant with a major accounting firm: he enjoys auditing, but is fed up with having to work with understaffed teams. So he decides to take a job in a corporate internal audit group, where he'll be part of a robust team. Although he has to travel and put in long hours from time to time, his life is more balanced than it was before, and he's generally pretty satisfied. Several years later, he may be told that he's being groomed to head up the entire internal audit group in the future, but that he can't be considered for that promotion unless he first works in divisional accounting overseas, and also serves in an accounting policy role at the corporate offices. If this accountant did his homework before coming on board, and is therefore aware of the corporation's penchant for rotating leadership candidates, he's fully prepared. Otherwise, it will come as a rather unsettling surprise.

## ⚊ Chapter One: Action Items ⚊

1. Visualize a day, a month, and a year of practice – activities, relationships with clients or patients, attributes of success or failure–at both your current professional services firm and at the corporation you're considering joining.

2. Think about what you truly enjoy about your current, day-to-day work and what you'd like to eliminate.

3. Make sure you have obtained enough information to understand fully what's involved in practice at the corporation. Ask to meet with others in similar positions in the organization—ideally, those who came from a background similar to yours—to help identify differences you might not have anticipated. Useful questions to ask include:

   a. What do you like best, and least, about in-house practice?

   b. What surprised you most about in-house practice, compared to practice at a firm?

   c. What has been the hardest thing for you to adapt to here?

4. List your priorities. Include columns for your current professional venue and for the corporate opportunity you're considering. This will help you thoroughly evaluate whether the new environment will be a good fit for you. For an attorney, the list might look like this:

| Factor | Current firm | In-house opportunity |
|---|---|---|
| Chance to be home most weekends | No | Somewhat |
| Achieve financial goals | Somewhat | Greater upside (if options hit big) but more risk (if options are worthless) |
| Interesting work | Yes | Uncertain |

# Evaluating an Employer: Corporate Culture Matters

One important factor that many professionals overlook when considering an in-house position is the culture of the new corporation (and division or team). Since what one may find appealing could be a complete turn-off to another, the goal here is not only to understand the culture, but also to determine—before you accept a new position—whether you'll be comfortable working within that culture.

We'll talk in a minute about how to assess corporate/division/team culture, but before we get there, it's essential that you first explore the corporation's track record on business integrity. Push beyond mere compliance with the law, and look for a robust commitment to ethical behavior. If a corporation has stumbled in this area, find out whether management has been changed in the aftermath, and whether they've now made a clear commitment to operating in a new way. It can be very satisfying to serve as part of the "clean-up" team that gets a corporation back on track. But be extremely cautious if your prospective employer has had some troubles but has made no visible efforts to change things. Reporting to an executive charged with a crime is very different from representing him as outside counsel. And no professional wants to be in the uncomfortable position of having to choose between being a whistleblower to regulators about illegal conduct or facing prison himself.

Once you're satisfied on the issue of business integrity, you can move on to considering the culture of the industry, the corporation, and the division where you would work. Use the following steps as an outline to help you through the process:

1. **The overall industry.** Is it growing? Stable? Troubled? Next, consider the fundamentals of the industry: What steps are involved in bringing products and services to customers? How are profits earned and measured? What external factors might be affecting the industry?

2. **The corporation's place in the industry.** Is it the largest? The most admired? The smallest? Scrappiest? Think of how this may impact the corporation's culture and business practices, as well as how it fits with your priorities.

3. **The corporation's aspirations.** You'll find these in the annual report to shareholders, on the corporation's website, and possibly in articles written about the company in trade and/or consumer publications. Is it looking to double its sales? Pare down? Improve the quality of its products or services? Enter emerging markets? As with Question 2, there are no right or wrong answers. What's important is that you assess how well the corporation's aspirations mesh with your priorities.

4. **Your physical location and your spot in the food chain.** Will you be at headquarters reporting to a senior leader, or working in a division or subsidiary?

5. **How decisions are made and communicated.** An executive who likes to make quick decisions and work independently may be happiest in a lean, entrepreneurial culture, while an executive who likes to thoroughly analyze issues, and make sure others see things her way before proceeding, may find a more formal environment suits her best. A leader just leaving the military for the corporate world may be more comfortable in a hierarchical culture where communications move through people of like rank, as opposed to a more flexible culture where it's typical for an executive to go straight to another's subordinate if that's faster.

6. **Special legal or cultural differences.** This is especially important if the corporation is headquartered in a location you aren't directly familiar with. For example, let's say you're a German lawyer and have just been offered a job at a German subsidiary of a US-based corporation. Although it's physically in Germany, that subsidiary will likely need to enforce a complex compliance system relating to the U.S. Foreign Corrupt Practices Act. Part of your job will be to help the local business team understand the importance of complying with that U.S. anti-bribery law, which can be very challenging when your competitors work for global companies that aren't subject to that law (or any similar laws).

## — Chapter Two: Action Items —

1. Be honest and clear with yourself about the environments you thrive in and that facilitate your best work, as well as those where you know you'd be unhappy. Don't allow yourself to be blinded by salary and other perks (unless you're 100 percent sure you won't regret your decision a few years down the line).

2. Talk to people on all levels of the corporation to make sure you understand:

   a. Tone at the top.

   b. How decisions are made.

   c. How employees relate to bosses, peers, and subordinates.

   d. Special cultural issues, such as those that inevitably exist at a subsidiary physically located in a different nation than the parent company.

3. Be sure to understand the personalities and work habits of those who would be in your chain of command, your peers, and your team.

# Evaluating an Employer: Due Diligence

Before deciding whether a prospective employer is right for you, you'll need to learn about its operational and financial strengths and challenges. You'll be able to gather important information from the company's Human Resources department, the search firm that made the connection, and the people you'll be working for in your new position. Be like a sponge: absorb every word.

But that's not all—you'll also need to do some independent research to dig up unbiased information (search firms, as well as the company's HR people and your likely future supervisors, all have a somewhat vested interest in painting a positive picture). Corporations have to make several important filings every year with the Securities and Exchange Commission (SEC). Read them. They're available free of charge at sec.gov in the EDGAR database):

- **10-K.** Read the "Business Description" to get an overview of the business. Read the "Management's Discussion and Analysis" to get a sense of financial drivers of past performance, as well as trends that may impact performance going forward. Read the contingency or litigation footnote to the financial statements to get a sense of legal and regulatory risks. Check the list of executive officers and read their biographies; these officers will be your peers or superiors, and you'll want to understand their backgrounds.

- **Proxy Statement.** Read the biographies of the Board of Directors. Since they're the ones who elect the officers and oversee management, a strong Board is important. Read the "Compensation Discussion and Analysis" to learn about the pay philosophy: is compensation performance-driven or seniority-based? If it's seniority-based, you'll want to know whether the company will count only your years with them, or whether they'll take into consideration your work elsewhere, which would put you on the same footing as others who have been practicing the same number of years.

Don't forget one of the simplest resources of all: Google the corporation, its products and services, and its leaders. Of course, not everything you read on the Web is true, but if you scan a good selection of articles from neutral sources, the overall information can provide insights into the public's perception of your prospective new employer.

Finally, get some informal feedback from people in your personal network. These could include former colleagues who currently work at the prospective employer, as well as friends who know current or past employees. Don't limit yourself to people on or near your position on the org chart. You may be able to get as much insight from an executive assistant as from an executive.

## ⏤ Chapter Three: Action Items ⏤

1. Read everything the corporation and the search firm provide.

2. Read key sections of the corporation's SEC filings.

3. Use the Web judiciously.

4. Use your network and gather information from people who have insights into all levels of the organization you're considering.

# Evaluating an Offer: Title and Level

E very corporation has its own hierarchy. Titles are much less indicative of compensation and standing in the corporation than they are in most professional services firms. For that reason, it's important to get beyond title to understand the true level of a particular position in the corporation you are thinking of joining.

First, carefully read the actual job description. If the person who last did the job is still working at the corporation (say, for example he/she has been promoted), it's also helpful to talk with him/her about the role.

Second, to truly determine the level of a position, one must consider how the position fits within the organization. For example, to an uninformed outsider, "Vice President–Finance" sounds like an important role. But as you'll see in the chart on the following page, the words that make up the title can mean very different things, depending on the corporation's structure.

| Corporation A | Corporation B | Corporation C |
|---|---|---|
| CEO | CEO | CEO |
| Executive Vice President & CFO | Executive Vice President & CFO | Executive Vice President & CFO |
| Vice President-Finance (1 incumbent) | Senior Vice President-Finance (5 incumbents) | Vice President-Finance (1 incumbent) |
| | Vice President-Finance (20 incumbents) | Group Vice President-Finance (3 incumbents) |
| | | Vice President-Finance (3 incumbents) |

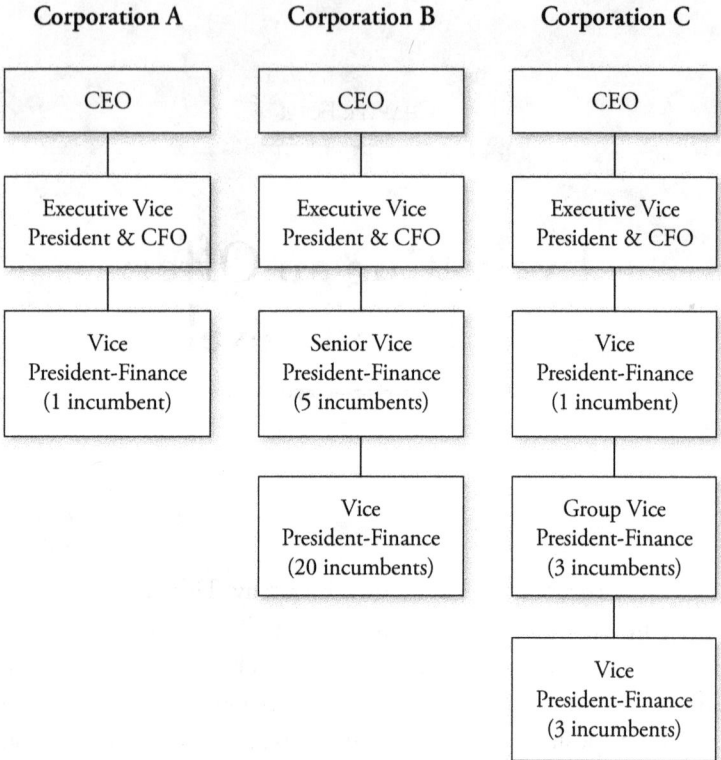

Third, find out where the division you'll be joining stands relative to other divisions within the organization. In some corporations, the operational division leadership outranks the corporate support division leadership, while in others, the finance division is more powerful than any of the operational divisions. In some cases this is truly a reflection of the corporate culture of the organization, but in others it reflects where the senior executive leading a division falls in the management chain of command. In the examples below, the Executive Vice Presidents and the Senior Vice Presidents all report to the CEO, but the Executive Vice Presidents have achieved higher compensation levels, more authority and more resources than the Senior Vice Presidents.

**Corporation A**

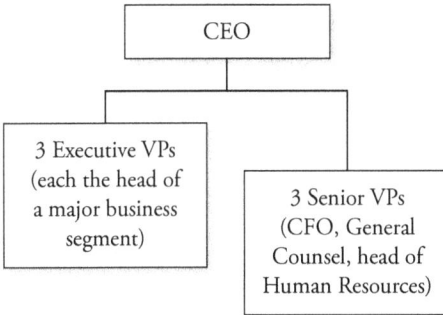

```
                    ┌──────────────┐
                    │     CEO      │
                    └──────────────┘
         ┌────────────────┴────────────────┐
┌──────────────────┐              ┌──────────────────┐
│ 3 Executive VPs  │              │ 3 Senior VPs     │
│ (each the head of│              │ (CFO, General    │
│ a major business │              │ Counsel, head of │
│ segment)         │              │ Human Resources) │
└──────────────────┘              └──────────────────┘
```

**Corporation B**

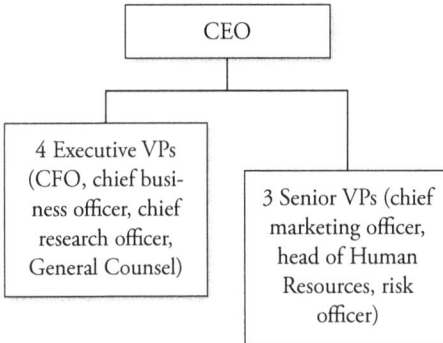

```
                    ┌──────────────┐
                    │     CEO      │
                    └──────────────┘
         ┌────────────────┴────────────────┐
┌──────────────────┐              ┌──────────────────┐
│ 4 Executive VPs  │              │ 3 Senior VPs (chief│
│ (CFO, chief busi-│              │ marketing officer,│
│ ness officer, chief│            │ head of Human    │
│ research officer,│              │ Resources, risk  │
│ General Counsel) │              │ officer)         │
└──────────────────┘              └──────────────────┘
```

Here are some useful questions to ask in order to make sure you truly understand where a particular position fits in a corporation:

- How many people are there in the chain of command between me and the CEO? (In case you're not familiar with typical corporate terminology, this is usually referred to as your "level;" for example, the CEO is Level 1, his direct reports are Level 2, their direct reports are Level 3, etc.).

- What is my supervisor's span of control (in other words, how many direct reports does he/she have), and what is my span of control?

- What is the size of my organization (all of your reports, direct and indirect) and my supervisor's organization (all of his direct and indirect reports)?

- How many other people have the same title in my department and throughout the entire corporation?

- Does everyone with the same title have the same authority, resources, and access to information? For example:

  ○ If there are five Deputy General Counsels who report to a General Counsel, can each one approve settlements up to the same dollar limit? Do they have the authority to select outside counsel as they wish?

  ○ If there are three Vice Presidents-Finance who report to a Chief Financial Officer, do they all receive earnings forecasts and alerts on material non-public developments in the business?

  ○ If there are two Co-Presidents, can each use the corporate aircraft to reach key meetings around the globe?

If people holding the same title are treated differently when it comes to authority, access to information, and resources, then it's very important that you understand whether or not you'll be in the group with the higher authority. If not, find out why, and what you'd need to do to achieve that higher level.

Finally, it's important that you understand other designations that may impact your position. One of these is membership on teams or committees.

Many companies have a committee made up of the most senior executives—usually half a dozen to a dozen—often called the Executive Management Team or Executive Leadership Committee. The structure of these groups varies greatly. At some corporations, all of the CEO's direct reports are members of the committee, while at others, some, such as the executives who lead support divisions, may be excluded. In yet a third version, an executive committee may include additional key executives who are not direct reports to the CEO. Membership on committees like these often comes with extra compensation and benefits, interaction with the Board of Directors, and participation in major strategic initiatives. Membership on such committees also may come with additional risks (such as a higher percentage of pay being subject to performance hurdles and clawbacks) or obligations (such as a higher required equity holdings levels and leadership of corporate civic initiatives).

Many companies also have teams made up of people below the senior executive level, such as an operational leadership team, a global leadership group, etc. These teams can have dozens or even hundreds of members, and typically confer extra compensation and benefits, special briefings on corporate initiatives, and additional career development opportunities. As you consider your career move, you'll need a clear understanding of what committees exist. How are members selected (Are certain positions automatically included? If not, does the CEO select them or do other senior executives designate members from among their direct reports? Is there a limit on the number of members from each division?). Learn whether you'll be a member, and benefits and obligations come with membership.

## — Chapter Four: Action Items —

1. Understand what your title signifies within the corporation.

2. Consider the authority, resources, and access to information you will have.

3. Factor in the organizational chart for your division and across divisions, to evaluate how your position will fit within the organization.

4. Also learn about other designations, such as membership on a leadership team or committee, which may confer additional resources and benefits.

# Evaluating an Offer: Compensation

Because executive compensation is so complex, it's important to carefully evaluate each component of the package you're considering. If you're not a compensation specialist, you may find this exercise somewhat boring, but learning the company's underlying philosophy and method for setting compensation will give you the framework you need to make a fully informed decision.

## Compensation Philosophy

Start by looking at the proposed compensation package in the context of the corporation's overall philosophy on compensation. Is compensation for all employees performance-based? If not, which groups of workers have seniority-based pay and which have performance-based pay? Does the corporation pay above-the-industry average to attract and retain the highest quality workers, or is there cost pressure that drives pay to the median or lower? The company's compensation philosophy is usually discussed in the proxy statement, which is available from the SEC's EDGAR database at sec.gov. Read it carefully. If the company's philosophy is to drive compensation down to the median and you're starting off above the median, it may be a while before you see a raise. At the same time, if the philosophy is to pay at the 75th percentile, and you're starting right at the median, there should be plenty of room for raises if you perform well.

Your prospective employer's compensation philosophy also will give you important insights about your subordinates and peers. At your professional services firm, you may be used to having high quality, well-paid colleagues, subordinate professionals and support staff. But as you consider your new team, think about whether the company's compensation philosophy will allow you access to the resources you'll need to attract top talent so you can build and maintain your own high quality team.

## Approval of Your Compensation Package

At public companies, regulations require that the Compensation Committee of the Board of Directors set compensation for senior executives. At some corporations, this committee sets the compensation of all officers. At other corporations, the CEO or the Human Resources executive approves the compensation for officers employees below the senior executive level, so long as overall costs stay within budget.

You need to know right up front whether your compensation and benefits package will need to be approved by the Compensation Committee of the Board. If so, you'll want to make sure that you and your advisors have fully evaluated all aspects of the package before the Human Resources team submits their recommendations to the Committee for approval. If you're considering any kind of executive level position, don't try to do this evaluation yourself.

You might, for example, be focused mostly on salary and bonus. But if you were to have an attorney look over the contract, he/she might point out that it's customary in your business to also receive change-in-control protection. If the Human Resources team had already submitted what you agreed to on your own, they might be reluctant to go back to the Committee to add the change-in-control protection. And even if they did agree to go back a second time, Compensation Committees don't particularly like to consider a package for the same new hire twice (and no executive wants to start off on a bad note with the Board).

## Base Pay

At the core of most corporations' pay packages is "base pay," or simply "salary." Base pay typically falls within a range, which is often tied to your level within the corporation. Salary ranges can and do overlap, so a senior person in a lower level might make more than a junior person in the level above. The following illustration shows hypothetical base pay ranges at a corporation where there are four levels of lawyers under an Executive Vice President, General Counsel.

| Deputy General Counsel (4 incumbents) | $300,000 to $450,000 |
|---|---|
| Senior Counsel (25 incumbents) | $220,000 to $335,000 |
| Counsel (55 incumbents) | $175,000 to $250,000 |
| Attorney (20 incumbents) | $125,000 to $180,000 |

## Annual and Long-Term Bonuses

Most corporations include some form of incentive pay to encourage strong team and/or individual performance. One frequent incentive pay instrument is an annual bonus. At most corporations, all employees are eligible to earn some type of annual bonus, but there may be a special program with different terms for executives.

In addition to the annual bonus, many corporations also offer a long-term incentive for the senior team. The number of executives eligible to receive long-term bonuses varies widely. At some corporations inclusion is automatic, based on level or title, while at other companies executives are individually selected to participate in the long-term program. The performance period also varies—often based on the product cycles in a particular industry—but periods of three to five years are most common.

When thinking about bonuses, there are several things you need to evaluate. First, what is the size of your bonus opportunity? This amount is often expressed as a percentage of base pay. For example, at one corporation, all Vice Presidents may have a target annual bonus opportunity of 50 percent of base pay, while at another, a Vice President's target opportunity may range from 30 to 60 percent of base pay. In still other corporations, the bonus opportunity may be expressed as a flat dollar amount based on title, salary range, or some other eligibility criterion.

Second, when thinking about bonus, be sure to ask how bonuses are paid (cash or equity), and whether there are clawbacks or holding periods (we'll talk about those below).

Third, when thinking about bonus, find out the metrics that the company uses to determine the bonus. Typically, there are corporate metrics that apply to everyone, such as increases in sales and earnings by specified percentages. There may also be metrics that apply only to your division. For example, that the law department holds outside counsel costs below a specified amount or that a sales division successfully launches a new product. Many corporations also include individual goals, which are typically set by the supervisor.

The mix of metrics also determines how the bonus is calculated. For example, at one corporation the corporate metrics may account for

50 percent of the annual bonus, divisional metrics for 30 percent, and individual metrics for the remaining 20 percent. At another, the corporate metrics may account for 100 percent of the bonus.

It's also important to understand any thresholds that might apply to the bonus, since they'll typically be very different than what you may have experienced at a professional services firm. In most professional services firms, individual performance (such a bringing in business or exceeding goals for billable hours) has a big impact on your bonus. At a corporation, however, the annual bonus plan typically would include a corporate metric, and perhaps also a divisional metric, on top of an individual performance metrics. If the plan includes thresholds for corporate and/or divisional metrics, and the thresholds are not met, then there is no bonus no matter how strong individual performance has been. Let's say at A Corporation, the corporate metric, which accounts for 60 percent of the total bonus package, targets an increase in sales of $20 million with no threshold. That means that even if the corporation doesn't meet its sales target, there might still be bonuses of up to 40 percent of target for hitting or exceeding divisional and individual metrics. But at B Corporation, say that the plan is the same except that there is a threshold on the corporate metric, that sales must increase by at least $10 million. If sales go up by only $4 million, no one would receive any annual bonus at all—even employees who delivered strong individual performance in a division that exceeded its divisional goals.

## Equity Awards

Annual equity awards (meaning stock, options, or other compensation instruments tied to stock) are typically provided to all salaried employees, or at least the higher-ranked salaried employees. Some corporations provide equity to all employees.

Corporations sometimes pay annual or long-term bonuses with equity. And they may also make special equity awards, such as signing or retention incentives, or to reward an individual or a team of employees for service on a particular project.

These are the most common types of equity awards:

- **Stock.** Shares of stock are provided to the employee.

- **Restricted Stock.** Employees receive shares of stock that come with certain restrictions. The restrictions may be time-based (the employee must remain employed for a set period of time—typically three to five years—or the stock will be forfeited). Or they may be performance-based (the stock award will be paid only if certain performance targets are achieved by the corporation (such as an increase in sales) and/or by the employee (such as receiving a performance rating of at least 3 on a 1–5 scale).

- **Stock Options.** A stock option is the right to purchase shares of stock at a specified price (called the "strike price" or the "option exercise price") within a set period of time (called the "exercise period"). Stock options have value only if the market price is higher than the strike price at the time when the option may be exercised. For example, let's say an employee at ACorp receives an option for 1,000 shares, with a strike price of $20 (the market price on the day the stock option was granted), exercisable for the period beginning three years after the grant and ending five years after the grant. The ACorp stock fluctuates from a low of $5 per share to a high of $60 per share over the exercise period. If the employee chooses to exercise and sell at $50 per share, here is how to calculate the compensation he/she would receive:

Gross receipts: $50 market price x 1,000 shares  =  $50,000
Less strike price: $20 per share x 1,000 shares  = –$20,000
    **Total payout**                             = **$30,000**

Keep in mind that the employee in this example will take home less than $30,000 because he/she will be required to pay federal and state income tax withholding at the time of exercise. Further, some option plans require that the employee pay an administrative charge upon the exercise of stock options, and broker fees upon sale of shares acquired by exercising the stock option.

Should the employee choose not to sell the shares after exercising of the stock option, and instead decides to hold the shares (either because the corporation imposes holding restrictions or because the employee believes the shares will be worth more later), projecting the value is even more complex. To start with, tax withholding is still due upon exercise. The amount of the tax is based on the spread between the strike price and the market price on the date of exercise. Some companies require that the employee pay the strike price and the withholding in cash at the date of exercise. Others will retain some of the shares to cover these costs, so that the employee doesn't have to come up with cash at the time of exercise. But as a result, the employee will end up with fewer shares after the exercise. Ultimately, the true compensation value to the executive won't be certain unless and until he/she sells the shares.

## Signing Bonuses

Corporations offer signing bonuses for a variety of reasons. Sometimes it's just a sweetener to induce the candidate to accept the offer. Other reasons include:

- to transition a candidate from his/her current compensation to the corporation's compensation structure;

- to make up for a compensation component from the current employer that the candidate would leave behind, such as unvested equity or the current year's bonus; or

- to compensate a candidate for anticipated higher cost of living or higher commuting costs.

Signing bonuses may offer cash, equity, or a combination; they may be paid up front or in installments spanning several years. Some signing bonuses include an obligation to repay, should the executive leave before a specified period of time has expired.

## A Word about Holding Requirements, Restrictions, and Clawbacks

Many companies have equity holding requirements for senior executives. For example, a vice president might be required to hold equity (in other words, buy and hold stock in the company) valued at the annual base salary, a senior vice president might be required to hold equity valued at three times base salary, and the CEO might be required to hold equity valued at eight times base salary. The executive is allowed a specified number of years to amass the required equity. There are various methods to calculate whether one is maintaining the threshold over time, since share prices rise and fall, and base salaries typically only rise.

Some companies impose holding restrictions on incentives and/or equity compensation. For example, cash earned under a long-term incentive plan or stock received upon the exercise of options might be required to be held in escrow (so the executive can't sell the stock or access the funds) for a specified period. That period might be as short as a year or extend until retirement. The compensation may also be subject to *clawback* (recapture by the corporation) in certain circumstances—for example, if financial statements for a prior period are restated.

# A Word about Disclosing Compensation and Benefits Information

If you are one of the most highly compensated employees at a corporation, information about your complete compensation and benefits package may be required to be published in the corporation's proxy statement (an annual document filed with the Securities and Exchange Commission) or other industry-specific regulatory filings.

These filings include rigid requirements about how to calculate the value of various types of compensation and benefits. In certain cases, the value disclosed in a filing will include contingent compensation that may never be received (such as the anticipated value of an incentive award which may pay out at zero if performance thresholds aren't met). As a result, the compensation and benefit totals in the filings often exceed the amounts taken home, as well as the gross compensation amounts shown on W-2 and other tax forms.

Because this information is generally considered public, it frequently ends up in newspapers and on blogs. It's always a good idea to warn one's spouse that such disclosures may be coming and to explain why the compensation available to be spent at home is lower (often significantly) than the amounts disclosed.

## Compensation Changes

A corporations makes changes in its compensation systems for any number of reasons: there may be a shift in the compensation philosophy or a need to control costs more tightly. There may be external pressures, such as demands from shareholders and the media to hold down executive compensation levels, or to eliminate certain features of compensation systems. Moreover, in recent years, governmental regulation has increasingly impacted compensation.

It's impossible to predict how and when the compensation policy of any given corporation may be changed. But it can be helpful to understand fluctuations in salary ranges, average payments under various bonus plans in the recent past, and major changes in the compensation system (whether voluntary or imposed by regulation) that have occurred over the past three to five years.

## ⟿ Chapter Five: Action Items ⟿

1. Regarding base salary:

   a. What is the proposed base?

   b. Where does it fall within the range for my position? What are the high and low for the range?

   c. What were the average increases in base salary for employees at my level for the past five years?

2. Regarding equity and incentive compensation:

   a. What types of annual awards are provided to employees at my level?

   b. What methods are used to calculate the amount of those awards?

   c. Over the past five years, how big (or small) have the awards paid to employees at my level been?

3. How is compensation adjusted? Is there an annual increase in base salary? How often are the limits for equity and incentive compensation adjusted? Has compensation been adjusted down, as well as up?

4. Am I eligible for a signing bonus? If yes, what are the terms and amount?

5. Are my equity awards and incentive compensation subject to holding thresholds, restrictions, or clawback?

6. Will the value of my compensation (including benefits) be disclosed—for example, in the corporation's proxy statement or in regulatory filings?

7. Are there any governmental limits on my compensation and benefits?

# Evaluating an Offer: Benefits

Almost all compensation packages include benefits that may provide considerable additional value. That's why it's so important not only to understand the benefits you would receive, but to calculate their actual value relative to your individual needs.

First, examine the broad-based "basic" benefits, which are usually the same as those provided to full-time employees—such as health insurance, a 401(k) defined contribution plan (which may or may not be matched by the employer), a defined benefit pension plan (less common in the current economy), and life insurance. Many corporations offer a "cafeteria plan" that allows employees to allocate before-tax dollars to pay for healthcare spending, childcare, and elder dependent care expenses.

Take time to read the fine print and understand its impact on you, given your particular situation and priorities. For example, the Human Resources department might tell you that the corporation has an excellent health insurance plan. That plan might be of great value to you if it covers most services from your physicians of choice, but of little or no value if it excludes or significantly limits access to them. Next, review the additional benefits you're likely to be offered—benefits which are provided to a limited number of higher-level employees. These might include:

- **A supplemental pension plan (often called a "SERP").** An important consideration for a SERP would be whether only actual service at the corporation is covered, or whether you may be able to negotiate credits for years worked in your field as well. (This accommodation is more common if you are walking away from a pension at your professional services firm by leaving before a vesting period has been achieved.)

- **Change-in-control benefits** (see Chapter Seven).

- **Executive life insurance.**

- **Financial and tax planning services.**

- **Home security systems at each residence.** This benefit is typical in industries that are targeted by violent activists.

- **A corporate-owned car or transportation allowance.**

- **The right to use corporate aircraft for business travel.** For very senior executives, this may also apply to specified levels of personal travel.

- **A reserved parking space.**

- **Relocation benefits.**

- **Executive physicals.**

- **Executive gym.**

- **Executive dining room.**

- **Memberships** (to everything from country clubs to professional societies) and subscriptions (for a private copy of business newspapers and journals).

Be sure you understand whether you will be eligible for these or any
other additional benefits. Eligibility can vary greatly by reporting
relationship, rank, title, salary range, and so on. Sometimes the offer
letter will say something like this: "…benefits customary for others
of your rank." So, if an additional benefit is important to you, but is
not specified in your offer letter or contract, be sure to ask about it.

In considering these additional benefits, you'll want to determine
whether they'll cause you to incur any tax liability (some companies also pay the tax on certain items, known as a "tax gross up"). If
so, you'll also want to understand how and when the tax on these
benefits will be calculated and collected.

Regulations can limit pay or provide recapture of pay in a particular industry or company, such as those companies which
took "TARP" bailout money during the financial crisis in the last
decade. You need to know whether any such regulations will apply.

## A Word about Licensing and Continuing Education Costs

Don't forget to ask whether professional licensing and continuing
education costs are paid by the corporation.

For lawyers, one corporation may pay for all bar dues in multiple
jurisdictions and provide generous travel budgets for attending
specialized continuing legal education programs of the lawyer's
choice. Another corporation might pay bar dues in only one juris-
diction, and expect the lawyers to meet continuing legal education requirements by attending in-house or free continuing legal
education programs.

For accountants, one corporation might pay for the study program to prepare for the CPA exam, while another might not—and might even expect the aspiring accountant to use a vacation day when he takes the exam. And there will be similar variations in reimbursing the costs of attending continuing professional education programs, as described above for lawyers.

The same goes for fees and uncompensated time for membership in professional societies, such as the American Medical Association, Conference Board, Financial Executives Institute, American Bar Association, Society of Governance Professionals, etc. One corporation might place a high priority on developing its professionals as thought leaders in their respective fields, and therefore pay for and encourage such memberships; another, believing that these activities bring little or no value, wouldn't pay dues or allow for paid time off.

## ⏤ Chapter Six: Action Items ⏤

1. What benefits are provided to all employees? Get a copy of the plans to check the actual value to you, considering such questions as whether your physicians of choice will be covered by the health insurance plan.

2. What special additional benefits are being offered?

3. What are the tax implications of the benefit package?

4. Will your compensation and benefits be disclosed, for example, to certain regulators or in the corporation's proxy statement?

5. Are there any governmental restrictions on your compensation and benefits?

# Evaluating an Offer:
# Change-in-Control Protection

At certain corporations, some level of basic change-in-control protection extends to all employees who have worked a specified minimum period of time. This benefit is paid when control of the corporation changes, such as in a merger or spin-off. In some cases, a simple change of ownership is all that's required to trigger the benefits, while in others, the employee's job must be eliminated or significantly changed (see discussion of "Timing of benefit—single and double triggers," below). This protection typically provides compensation pursuant to a formula. For rank and file employees, that might be something like two weeks base pay for each year worked, with a minimum of three months base pay and a maximum of two years base pay. Sometimes the value of the annual incentive is also included.

Many corporations provide executives with contractual change-in-control protection, which is more significant than the broad-based protections. One reason for this is that the senior team is the most "at risk" because no company needs two CEOs, CFOs, or General

Counsels. A number of key features may be provided in senior-level change-in-control protections, including:

- **Amount of the benefit.** Typically, executives receive two or three times their annual salary and annual incentive. Sometimes the value of long-term incentives, and/or equity awards, is included.

- **Performance-based awards**. Typically, if employment terminates in the middle of a performance period, the award opportunity is forfeited. However, if employment terminates because of a change-in-control, there is usually some payment for that performance period, but—as with so many details of corporate compensation—how the payment is calculated, and when it is paid, varies. In some instances, it's a pro-rata payment distributed at the end of the performance period. Thus, if a change-in-control occurs in June for an annual plan with a calendar year performance period, then at year-end when the performance metrics are known, the executive would get half of the bonus because he worked for half of the performance period. In other cases, the company will apply a formula to determine the amount of a payout to be made at the time of the change-in-control. For example, in the same situation as discussed above, where a change-in-control occurs in June for an annual plan with a calendar year performance period, the executive would receive an award at the time of the change-in-control, with the amount of the award being equal to the target for the annual bonus.

- **Equity.**

    - **Stock options.** In most cases, the period during which stock options can be exercised ends when employment terminates. This means that if the options haven't vested by the change-in-control date, and the executive loses his job on that date, the options can't be exercised at all. In that instance, the executive loses any chance of realizing value from the options. However, with change-in-control protection, vesting of stock options may be accelerated to coincide with the change-in-control. In addition, the original exercise period may be protected, thus allowing the executive to continue to exercise the options until their original expiration date, instead of the date on which his/her employment terminates.

○ **Restricted stock.** The holding period for time-based restricted stock may also be accelerated, so that restricted stock won't be forfeited, regardless of whether or not employment is terminated.

- **SERP**. Additional service credits may be added to the supplemental pension so that the benefit is calculated as if the executive had worked several additional years.

- **Other benefits.** Continued medical insurance, life insurance, availability of an office for several years, outplacement services, and other benefits may be included.

- **Timing of the benefit—single and double triggers.** Executives sometimes receive change-in-control benefits when control of the corporation changes (known as a "single trigger"); in other cases the payment is received only if the executive's position is eliminated or diminished, such as when the CEO becomes the COO after a change-in-control (known as a "double trigger").

- **Tax gross up payment.** Executives may owe additional taxes on the value provided through the change-in-control protections, including special excise taxes. Some companies provide an additional payment to make the executive whole for the amount of the special excise tax liability.

Many corporations also provide executives with severance protection. The formula works the same way as the change-in-control. Severance protection is paid when the executive leaves:

- **At the Company's request, before the end of his/her contract period for any reason other than "cause."** "Cause" is typically defined in the contract as breaking laws or harming the corporation intentionally.

- **Of his/her own volition following an event of "good reason."** The definition of "good reason" may include events such as demotion, change of title, change in reporting structure or level within the corporation, or change in function. The definition is often a point of intense negotiation, and it's important to think carefully about what parameters are important to you. Let's look at the protection offered by two different definitions of "good reason" in an example. Say you are the CFO of a publicly traded company and you report directly to the Chairman and CEO. The company takes a division and drops it down into a wholly owned subsidiary. At that time, you are made CFO of the subsidiary and someone else is named CFO of the company. The larger company offers to let you continue as CFO of the subsidiary at your old rate of pay, but you'd report to the CFO of the parent company. At first glance, the following definition of "good reason" may seem to offer adequate protection:

  > *"Good reason" means the executive's title is changed to other than CFO (or a more senior title upon promotion, such as COO or CEO) or his total compensation is diminished.*

If you are just a few years away from retirement and have no aspirations of attaining a subsequent, more senior, position, the above definition may be acceptable, as you may be willing to continue working after you are moved to serve as CFO of the subsidiary. However, if you had aspirations of becoming a CEO, that definition might be problematic, as the position being offered is a step backward from where you are now. You might be better served by a definition of "good reason" that would allow you to decline the offer, receive full severance, and spend your time locating a more suitable position elsewhere. Such a definition might read:

> *"Good reason" means any of the following: (i) the executive's role is changed to other than CFO (or a more senior title upon promotion, such as COO or CEO) of the public company that is the parent entity; (ii) the executive is no longer a direct report to the Chairman and CEO of the public company that is the parent entity; or (iii) the executive's total compensation is diminished.*

Both severance payments and the tax gross up have become controversial with investors. As a result, some corporations have agreed not to provide these protections in future executive contracts. Should you be considering a great job where these protections are not provided for any reason, I strongly suggest that you be particularly diligent in analyzing with your advisors whether the company is a takeover target, how high the turnover is for your position, etc.

## — Chapter Seven: Action Items —

1. Consider what protection you are likely to need and compare that to what's being offered:

   a. How likely is a change-in-control, given the size of the corporation and the nature of the industry?

   b. What is the average tenure of executives at your level? (For example, if the Board shows little patience and turns over the executive suite often, severance may be a more important consideration than in a situation where most executives stay a decade or more.)

# A Word about Advisors

It's a heady feeling to be recruited hard for a position. It can be easy to fall into the trap of viewing the situation through rose-colored glasses, particularly if you're feeling restless in your current position, or are out of work.

As you consider an in-house offer, chances are that, in addition to your prospective supervisor, several other professionals will be involved in recruiting you. These would likely include a search firm expert and an executive from the corporation's Human Resources department. Because all of these folks will have valuable insights and perspectives, it's very important that you listen to and learn from them. They have a clear interest in putting the right person in the job. However, the party they ultimately must please is the corporation, not you. So you'll also want to consult others, to make sure you have evaluated all important factors thoroughly before accepting an offer.

It's helpful to have a small group of trusted advisors who have no interest in the corporation that's recruiting you. Over the years, I've been fortunate to have put together a "career cabinet" made up of several former colleagues, bosses, and clients, as well as an executive coach who knows me well. Each "cabinet member" is willing to ask tough questions and help me make sure I have fully considered all relevant factors when making a decision to accept or reject an offer.

Beyond the career cabinet—particularly if you'll be an officer or executive of a corporation, one key advisor should be an attorney whose specialty is executive employment matters. These experts are familiar with what is standard in the marketplace for positions similar to yours, so they add benchmarking strength to your team, as well a 360° view on the various compensation instruments and contract provisions being offered to you. Furthermore, they will have crafted creative solutions to many common issues that may arise in negotiating executive employment arrangements. Some executives involve this expert attorney directly in negotiating the terms of their employment with the prospective employer; others simply factor in the expert's advice when making decisions. Certain corporations will reimburse an executive for this expense as part of the signing package. However, even if you're not going to be reimbursed, I believe that getting advice from a seasoned expert is well worth the expense.

Another key person to consult is your tax advisor. Professionals who received only cash compensation in the past will want to understand how and when equity compensation is taxed. Tax professionals also can help you craft a tax-planning strategy for dealing with signing bonuses and other compensation features that are different from the compensation package you received at your professional services firm.

At the end of the day, however, you're the one who must decide how an offer stacks up against your personal needs and objectives. The role of your career cabinet, attorney, and tax adviser is to help you make sure you've considered every possible perspective so your decision will be well-informed.

## ⏤ Chapter Eight: Action Items ⏤

1. Consider all information from the corporation, including:

   a. Your prospective supervisor; and

   b. The corporation's human resources contact.

2. Consider all information from the search firm professional.

3. Retain your own attorney who specializes in executive compensation and employment matters.

4. Retain your own tax advisor.

5. Assemble your own "career cabinet" of people who know you well and understand the corporate world. Ask them to test your assumptions and make sure you are considering all relevant perspectives.

# Contracts, Offer Letters, and More

Some corporations provide employment contracts to all employees of a certain level, and others take pride in having no contracts—even for the CEO.

Either way, you'll most likely receive an offer letter, which job seekers sometimes confuse with a contract. The offer letter is often contingent on completion of certain events (such as background checks and drug testing) and, depending on a variety of other factors, may not create an enforceable obligation of the corporation.

Pay close attention, in order to fully understand the details of the compensation being offered. For example, if the corporation includes a 6 percent employer match under the 401(k) plan, useful details would include:

- Whether the match vests immediately.

- Whether the match is automatically invested in company stock, as opposed to the investment fund(s) of your choice.

- Restrictions on withdrawing (or borrowing) your own contributions and the match during your employment.

Benefit plans often include provisions that impact your compensation and the terms of employment. For example, even if change-in-control protection is not covered in a contract, there is typically an executive change-in-control plan that includes the protections provided to executives (see Chapter 7 for more on this). Your offer letter may state that you will have coverage under that plan at two times salary and bonus. However, you'll also want to review the plan details to make sure you understand how much you'll be entitled to, and when. Details that would be relevant in this example include:

Whether the change-in-control protection is single triggered (meaning that you will receive the benefit if there is a change-in-control), or double triggered (meaning that you *won't* receive the benefit after a change-in-control unless your position is also eliminated as a result of the change-in-control).

- Whether you will receive an excise tax gross up.

- What bonus amount will be used in the formula? Two options commonly used are (1) the highest bonus actually paid over the past five years, or, (2) the target annual bonus for the year in which the merger closes.

- As mentioned in Chapter 8, it's very important that you have a lawyer review the benefit plans, as well as all other documents that will impact your career with the corporation. Don't hesitate to ask for copies. As discussed in Chapter 3, you can get most of these documents, free of charge, from the Securities and Exchange Commission website at sec.gov. On that site, go to the EDGAR database and look for the corporation's documents. Typically, compensation and benefit plans are exhibits to the corporation's filings on Form 10-K or Form 8-K.

## ⏤ Chapter Nine: Action Items ⏤

1. What documentation is your prospective employer providing? An offer letter? An employment contract? Get copies in advance, and leave yourself plenty of time to review them on your own, and with your advisors.

2. Review other plans and material that may contain terms and conditions that would impact you. Make sure you have enough information to fully value what you will receive.

3. Be vigilant about the details of severance and change-in-control protections.

# Getting Off to a Good Start

Once you've accepted an offer, you still have a bit more home-work to do before you show up for your first day on the job:

- Read the 10-K, and all other company information you have received, in detail.

- Learn all of the corporation's products. Here's an example of how this can be important: on your first day as in-house counsel at a food company, it would be bad form when break time comes, to start unwrapping a snack bar you brought from home that just happens to be a competitor's product.

- Study photographs on the corporation's website, proxy statement and annul report to enable you to recognize senior executives and board members on sight. Memorize their bios.

Once at your new job, do a lot of listening. Absorb as much information and learn as many protocols as you can. Try not to mention your past employer too frequently. And unless you're specifically hired as a change agent, be judicious about suggesting change.

Typically, there will be a new employees' orientation, where you'll receive general information about your new employer's business, practices, and systems. For senior executives, these are often a series of 1-on-1 sessions.

Don't be shy about introducing yourself at meetings or asking for the names and functions of others.

Do your best to meet everyone in your chain of command, your team, and your peers as soon as possible.

Ask for background and supplemental information on projects. More often than not, an employee who's been on the job for a while is a walking storehouse of useful historical information, but it may never cross his mind to share it with a newcomer. And that kind of information could be critical in putting a project in context for you. For example, say, you're a compensation specialist and you've been asked to draft a new equity incentive plan. You notice that the current equity incentive plan, unlike most stock incentive plans, doesn't include stock options as one of the equity compensation instruments that may be issued. If you don't ask for background, you might include stock options as one of the compensation instruments available in the new plan. But if you did ask, you might learn that the company had fired an executive over stock option backdating several years earlier. As a consequence, the Chair of the Board's Compensation Committee had directed that no more stock options would be issued to the executive team, in order to calm the waters with disgruntled investors. This additional piece information would alert you to ask your supervisor for guidance about the appropriate time and manner to re-introduce the subject of stock options.

If, by the end of your first week on the job, you haven't had the opportunity to learn the corporation's mission and values, the key elements of the corporation's strategic plan, your boss' goals for the current year, and his/her thoughts on *your* initial goal(s), ***ask!*** This knowledge is vital; it will give you the framework you need to prioritize projects, and a broad perspective as you study background materials.

Be positive. Give yourself time to learn a new way of practicing your profession, a way which fits well with the culture of your new employer. As with any major change, there will be days when you question whether you made the right decision. In most instances, it will take six to twelve months of experience to fully understand and feel comfortable in your new environment.

## — Chapter Ten: Action Items —

1. Learn as much as possible about your new corporation and its leadership before you start.

2. Once on board, get a sense of the lay of the land before suggesting or implementing change. Look at the big picture.

3. When starting a new project, be sure to evaluate the full context. Do extra work to be sure you understand how the project fits within the bigger picture (long-range strategic plan, mission, goals). Ask about background details that others may know, but have simply not realized you need to know, too.

4. Get to know others and their roles.

5. Be positive.

# A Checklist of Factors to Consider When Going In-House

1. Evaluate whether the nature of in-house practice—with no particular corporation in mind—truly meshes with what you like and don't like about your current, day-to-day work.

2. Consider whether the culture of the particular corporation you're considering is a good fit for you.

3. Perform your due diligence about the industry, the corporation, and the senior management team.

4. Look beyond the title of the position you're considering, so that you fully understand the level being offered.

5. Analyze the compensation.

6. Analyze the benefits.

7. Consider how likely it is that you will need change-in-control protection and severance protection. Evaluate all details of what your prospective employer is offering.

8. Consult your own advisors.

9. Thoroughly evaluate your offer letter, contract, and other terms of employment. Watch for small details, as well as major terms.

10. If you decide to move in-house, lay the foundation for a good start by doing your homework before your first day on the job, and over the first year continue to study everything you can that will help you learn your role .

# About the Author

Susan Ellen Wolf is a securities lawyer and corporate governance expert. A graduate of Emory University and The George Washington University Law School, Susan has held in-house positions at several corporations, including Schering-Plough (now Merck), The Coca-Cola Company, Delta Air Lines, Constellation Energy, and Continental Telephone Company (now Verizon).

Susan is active in professional associations and has served as Chairman of the Society of Corporate Secretaries and Governance Professionals; Co-Chair of the American Bar Association Committee on Securities, Commodities, & Exchanges; and as a Board member at the Council of Institutional Investors. Susan is currently a member of the Board of Advisors of the Temple University School of Medicine.

Over time, Susan began keeping a journal of questions asked by colleagues considering a move from a professional firm to a corporation. This book is a distillation of the common themes included in the journal over a 25 year period.

# Acknowledgments

Thanks to the many people who made this book possible:

The Sisters of the Holy Names of Jesus and Mary, who encouraged me to journal-keep during my years at the Academy of Holy Names in Tampa, Florida.

Fred Hassan, who encouraged me and so many others to follow our dreams.

Karen Ling, a talented human resources executive and an expert compensation attorney, who took time from her busy life to offer insights and perspectives.

Barbara Greene, who taught me the power of positive thinking.

Anne Bucci, who helped with manuscript preparation.

Charlotte Lee, who encouraged me to try new endeavors as I was finding my professional way, after losing a job I loved in connection with a merger. Charlotte also introduced me to Armin Brott, a seasoned author, who guided me, as a first time author, through the many processes and decisions involved in bringing a book to market. And Rick Soldin, who did the cover and interior design.